EMMANUEL JOSEPH

The Quiet Revolution, How Solitude, Curiosity, and Resilience Redefine Modern Life

Copyright © 2025 by Emmanuel Joseph

All rights reserved. No part of this publication may be reproduced, stored or transmitted in any form or by any means, electronic, mechanical, photocopying, recording, scanning, or otherwise without written permission from the publisher. It is illegal to copy this book, post it to a website, or distribute it by any other means without permission.

First edition

This book was professionally typeset on Reedsy.
Find out more at reedsy.com

Contents

1	Chapter 1: The Power of Solitude	1
2	Chapter 2: Curiosity as a Catalyst	3
3	Chapter 3: The Resilience Within	5
4	Chapter 4: Redefining Modern Life	7
5	Chapter 5: Embracing Change	9
6	Chapter 6: The Art of Reflection	11
7	Chapter 7: The Pursuit of Passion	13
8	Chapter 8: The Balance of Work and Play	14
9	Chapter 9: The Role of Mindfulness	15
10	Chapter 10: The Gift of Gratitude	17
11	Chapter 11: The Wisdom of Simplicity	19
12	Chapter 12: The Beauty of Nature	20
13	Chapter 13: The Strength of Community	22
14	Chapter 14: The Influence of Technology	24
15	Chapter 15: The Practice of Self-Compassion	26
16	Chapter 16: The Journey of Lifelong Learning	28
17	Chapter 17: The Quiet Revolution	30

1

Chapter 1: The Power of Solitude

In the hustle and bustle of our modern world, the idea of solitude often carries a negative connotation. Yet, solitude is more than just being alone—it's about reconnecting with oneself. Away from the constant noise and distraction, we find a space where creativity and reflection thrive. The essence of solitude is not loneliness but a conscious choice to detach, to unwind, and to delve into the depths of our own minds. Here, we can confront our fears, explore our dreams, and rediscover our passions without external influences.

Solitude allows us to recharge our mental and emotional batteries. In solitude, we become better at managing our emotions and understanding our responses to different stimuli. It's a quiet force that fosters resilience. By learning to be comfortable with ourselves, we build the capacity to face life's challenges with confidence. Instead of relying on others for validation or support, we develop an internal fortitude that helps us weather any storm. Solitude teaches us to be our own best friend and counselor.

Moreover, solitude nurtures curiosity. When we are alone, our minds wander freely. Questions arise, and we seek answers. This unfettered curiosity fuels innovation and learning. In solitude, many groundbreaking ideas and profound realizations have come to life. We can explore the corners of our minds, ask the big questions, and find ourselves lost in the wonder of discovery. Solitude is the birthplace of curiosity, a place where ideas germinate and grow without constraints.

Ultimately, embracing solitude is about redefining our relationship with ourselves and the world around us. It's a quiet revolution that challenges the status quo of constant connectivity and social validation. By valuing solitude, we step into a new paradigm where introspection and self-awareness take precedence. This shift empowers us to live more authentically and to pursue our passions with clarity and purpose. The journey begins with a single step into the quiet sanctuary of our own minds.

2

Chapter 2: Curiosity as a Catalyst

Curiosity is the engine that drives progress and innovation. It is the force behind every question, every exploration, and every discovery. From the simplest wonders of childhood to the most profound inquiries of scientists and philosophers, curiosity propels us forward. It's the spark that ignites the flames of knowledge and understanding, pushing us to seek out new horizons and challenge the boundaries of what we know.

In our modern world, curiosity is often overshadowed by the need for quick answers and instant gratification. However, true curiosity requires patience and a willingness to embrace uncertainty. It encourages us to delve deeper, to ask "why" and "how," and to explore the unknown with an open mind. This mindset fosters critical thinking and creativity, enabling us to approach problems from different angles and find innovative solutions.

Curiosity also plays a crucial role in personal growth and self-discovery. When we allow ourselves to be curious, we open up to new experiences, ideas, and perspectives. This openness leads to a richer, more fulfilling life, as we continuously learn and evolve. It helps us break free from the constraints of routine and familiarity, encouraging us to take risks and venture into uncharted territory. In doing so, we discover our true potential and uncover hidden talents and passions.

Moreover, curiosity strengthens our connections with others. By being genuinely interested in the world around us and the people we encounter, we foster empathy and understanding. We become better listeners, more engaged in conversations, and more attuned to the needs and experiences of those around us. This deepened connection enhances our relationships and fosters a sense of community and belonging. Curiosity, in essence, bridges the gap between ourselves and the world, enriching our lives in countless ways.

3

Chapter 3: The Resilience Within

Resilience is the ability to adapt and bounce back in the face of adversity. It's a crucial trait that allows us to navigate the inevitable challenges and setbacks that life presents. While resilience is often thought of as a natural trait, it can be developed and strengthened through experience and intentional effort. By cultivating resilience, we build the capacity to persevere and thrive, even in the most difficult circumstances.

One of the key components of resilience is a positive mindset. This doesn't mean ignoring or downplaying difficulties but rather approaching them with a sense of optimism and determination. A resilient mindset recognizes that setbacks are a part of life and that each challenge is an opportunity for growth and learning. By focusing on solutions and maintaining a sense of hope, we can overcome obstacles and emerge stronger and more capable.

Another important aspect of resilience is the ability to cope with stress. Life's challenges often come with a significant amount of stress, and learning to manage this stress is essential for maintaining our well-being. Effective coping strategies, such as mindfulness, exercise, and social support, can help us stay grounded and maintain a sense of balance. By developing these skills, we can better navigate the ups and downs of life and remain resilient in the face of adversity.

Resilience also involves a strong sense of purpose and meaning. When we have a clear sense of our values and goals, we are better equipped to persevere through difficult times. This sense of purpose provides a guiding light, helping us stay focused and motivated even when the going gets tough. By aligning our actions with our values and staying true to our goals, we can build a resilient foundation that supports us through life's challenges.

4

Chapter 4: Redefining Modern Life

In a world that is constantly evolving, redefining modern life requires us to embrace new perspectives and approaches. The rapid pace of technological advancement and societal change presents both opportunities and challenges. To navigate this ever-changing landscape, we must be adaptable, open-minded, and willing to question the status quo. By doing so, we can create a more fulfilling and meaningful life that aligns with our values and aspirations.

One of the key ways to redefine modern life is to prioritize meaningful connections and relationships. In an age of digital communication and social media, it's easy to become disconnected from the people around us. By making a conscious effort to cultivate genuine, in-person connections, we can create a stronger sense of community and support. This not only enhances our well-being but also fosters a deeper sense of belonging and purpose.

Another important aspect of redefining modern life is to focus on personal growth and self-discovery. In a world that often emphasizes external achievements and material success, it's essential to take the time to explore our inner selves. By engaging in activities that nurture our passions, interests, and talents, we can create a more balanced and fulfilling life. This journey of self-discovery allows us to align our actions with our values and create a life that is true to who we are.

Moreover, redefining modern life involves embracing a mindset of continuous learning and curiosity. In a rapidly changing world, staying informed and adaptable is crucial. By cultivating a love for learning and a willingness to explore new ideas, we can remain resilient and open to new opportunities. This mindset enables us to navigate the complexities of modern life with confidence and grace, continually growing and evolving along the way.

5

Chapter 5: Embracing Change

Change is an inevitable part of life, and learning to embrace it is essential for personal growth and resilience. While change can be daunting, it also presents opportunities for new experiences, learning, and self-discovery. By adopting a mindset that welcomes change, we can navigate the twists and turns of life with grace and confidence.

One of the first steps to embracing change is to shift our perspective. Instead of viewing change as a threat, we can see it as an opportunity for growth. This shift in mindset allows us to approach change with curiosity and optimism, rather than fear and resistance. By focusing on the potential benefits and opportunities that change can bring, we can harness its power to propel us forward.

Another important aspect of embracing change is to cultivate flexibility and adaptability. In a rapidly changing world, the ability to adjust and adapt is crucial. This involves being open to new ideas, willing to take risks, and ready to pivot when necessary. By developing these skills, we can better navigate the uncertainties of life and remain resilient in the face of change.

Moreover, embracing change involves letting go of the past and being present in the moment. Clinging to old habits, beliefs, and routines can hold us back from experiencing the full potential of what change has to offer. By releasing our attachment to the past and staying present, we can fully engage with the opportunities that change brings. This mindset allows us to move forward with a sense of clarity and purpose, embracing the new possibilities that lie ahead.

6

Chapter 6: The Art of Reflection

Reflection is a powerful tool for personal growth and self-awareness. By taking the time to reflect on our experiences, thoughts, and emotions, we can gain valuable insights and learn from our past. Reflection allows us to process our experiences, understand our reactions, and make informed decisions about our future.

One of the key benefits of reflection is that it helps us make sense of our experiences. In the hustle and bustle of daily life, it's easy to get caught up in the moment and lose sight of the bigger picture. Reflection provides us with the opportunity to step back and see our experiences in a broader context. This perspective allows us to identify patterns, recognize our strengths and weaknesses, and make more informed choices.

Another important aspect of reflection is that it fosters self-awareness. By regularly reflecting on our thoughts and emotions, we become more attuned to our inner selves. This self-awareness enables us to understand our motivations, desires, and fears. It also helps us identify areas for growth and improvement, allowing us to take proactive steps towards becoming our best selves.

Moreover, reflection can enhance our relationships with others. By reflecting on our interactions and behaviors, we can gain a better understanding of how we relate to the people around us. This insight allows us to communicate more effectively, resolve conflicts, and build stronger connections. Reflection, in essence, helps us become more empathetic and compassionate, improving our relationships and fostering a sense of community.

7

Chapter 7: The Pursuit of Passion

Passion is the driving force behind a fulfilling and meaningful life. It's the fire that fuels our creativity, motivates us to pursue our dreams, and inspires us to overcome challenges. By identifying and nurturing our passions, we can create a life that is rich with purpose and satisfaction.

The first step in the pursuit of passion is to explore our interests and curiosities. This involves being open to new experiences, trying different activities, and paying attention to what excites and energizes us. By experimenting with various pursuits, we can discover our true passions and uncover hidden talents.

Once we have identified our passions, it's important to nurture and cultivate them. This involves dedicating time and effort to our chosen pursuits, continually learning and growing in our areas of interest. By investing in our passions, we can develop a deep sense of expertise and mastery, which brings a sense of fulfillment and accomplishment.

Moreover, the pursuit of passion requires perseverance and resilience. Pursuing our dreams often involves facing obstacles and setbacks. However, by maintaining a steadfast commitment to our passions, we can overcome these challenges and continue moving forward. This resilience not only strengthens our resolve but also deepens our connection to our passions, making the journey all the more rewarding.

8

Chapter 8: The Balance of Work and Play

Finding a balance between work and play is essential for a healthy and fulfilling life. While hard work and dedication are important, so too is the need for relaxation, recreation, and leisure. By striking a balance between these two aspects of life, we can maintain our well-being and enjoy a more harmonious existence.

One of the key components of achieving balance is setting boundaries. This involves creating clear distinctions between work and leisure time, ensuring that one does not encroach on the other. By establishing boundaries, we can protect our personal time and prevent burnout, allowing us to be more productive and focused when we are working.

Another important aspect of balance is prioritizing self-care. This involves making time for activities that nurture our physical, mental, and emotional well-being. Whether it's exercise, hobbies, or spending time with loved ones, self-care activities provide us with the necessary rejuvenation to tackle our responsibilities with renewed energy and enthusiasm.

Moreover, finding balance requires being present in the moment. In our fast-paced world, it's easy to get caught up in the demands of work and forget to enjoy the simple pleasures of life. By practicing mindfulness and being fully engaged in whatever we are doing, we can create a more balanced and fulfilling life. This presence allows us to savor our experiences and make the most of both our work and leisure time.

9

Chapter 9: The Role of Mindfulness

Mindfulness is the practice of being fully present and engaged in the current moment. It's a powerful tool for managing stress, enhancing well-being, and cultivating a deeper connection to ourselves and the world around us. By incorporating mindfulness into our daily lives, we can create a more balanced and fulfilling existence.

One of the key benefits of mindfulness is its ability to reduce stress and promote relaxation. By focusing on the present moment, we can let go of worries about the past and future. This shift in attention allows us to experience a sense of calm and clarity, making it easier to navigate the challenges of daily life. Mindfulness also helps us recognize and manage our emotions, preventing them from overwhelming us.

Another important aspect of mindfulness is its impact on our overall well-being. Regular mindfulness practice has been shown to improve physical health, mental clarity, and emotional resilience. By paying attention to our thoughts, feelings, and bodily sensations, we can become more attuned to our needs and take proactive steps to care for ourselves. This heightened awareness promotes a greater sense of balance and harmony in our lives.

Moreover, mindfulness enhances our relationships with others. By being fully present and attentive in our interactions, we can create deeper connections and foster empathy and understanding. This presence allows us to listen more effectively, respond with compassion, and build stronger, more meaningful relationships. Mindfulness, in essence, helps us engage with the world in a more authentic and wholehearted way.

10

Chapter 10: The Gift of Gratitude

Gratitude is a powerful practice that can transform our perspective and enhance our overall well-being. By focusing on the positive aspects of our lives and expressing appreciation for them, we can cultivate a sense of joy and contentment. Gratitude helps us recognize the abundance in our lives and fosters a mindset of positivity and resilience.

One of the key benefits of gratitude is its ability to improve our mental and emotional health. Regularly practicing gratitude has been shown to reduce stress, increase happiness, and enhance overall life satisfaction. By shifting our focus from what we lack to what we have, we can create a more optimistic and positive outlook. This mindset allows us to navigate life's challenges with greater ease and resilience.

Another important aspect of gratitude is its impact on our relationships. By expressing appreciation for the people in our lives, we can strengthen our connections and foster a sense of mutual support and understanding. Gratitude helps us recognize the value of our relationships and the positive impact that others have on our lives. This recognition fosters a sense of community and belonging, enhancing our overall well-being.

Moreover, gratitude promotes a sense of purpose and meaning. By acknowledging and appreciating the positive aspects of our lives, we can create a deeper connection to our values and goals. This sense of purpose provides a guiding light, helping us stay focused and motivated even in challenging times. Gratitude, in essence, helps us align our actions with our values and create a more fulfilling and meaningful life.

11

Chapter 11: The Wisdom of Simplicity

In a world that often values complexity and busyness, embracing simplicity can be a powerful way to create a more balanced and fulfilling life. Simplicity involves focusing on what truly matters and letting go of unnecessary distractions and clutter. By simplifying our lives, we can create more space for the things that bring us joy and fulfillment.

One of the key benefits of simplicity is its ability to reduce stress and promote well-being. By removing unnecessary distractions and focusing on what truly matters, we can create a sense of calm and clarity. This shift in focus allows us to experience a greater sense of peace and contentment, making it easier to navigate the challenges of daily life.

Another important aspect of simplicity is its impact on our relationships. By simplifying our lives, we can create more time and space for meaningful connections with others. This focus on relationships fosters a sense of community and belonging, enhancing our overall well-being. Simplicity also allows us to be more present and attentive in our interactions, creating deeper and more meaningful connections.

Moreover, simplicity promotes a sense of purpose and clarity. By focusing on what truly matters, we can align our actions with our values and goals. This sense of purpose provides a guiding light, helping us stay focused and motivated even in challenging times. Simplicity, in essence, helps us create a more balanced and fulfilling life that is true to who we are.

12

Chapter 12: The Beauty of Nature

Nature has a profound impact on our well-being and sense of connection to the world around us. By spending time in nature, we can experience a sense of peace, wonder, and inspiration. Nature provides a sanctuary where we can reconnect with ourselves and find solace from the demands of daily life.

One of the key benefits of spending time in nature is its ability to reduce stress and promote relaxation. The natural environment has a calming effect on our minds and bodies, helping us feel more grounded and centered. By immersing ourselves in nature, we can let go of worries and distractions, allowing us to experience a sense of tranquility and rejuvenation.

Another important aspect of nature is its ability to inspire creativity and wonder. The beauty and diversity of the natural world can spark our imagination and ignite our sense of curiosity. By exploring nature, we can discover new perspectives and ideas, fostering a sense of creativity and innovation. Nature, in essence, provides a source of inspiration that can enrich our lives and fuel our passions.

Moreover, spending time in nature enhances our sense of connection and belonging. By experiencing the beauty and harmony of the natural world, we can develop a deeper appreciation for the interconnectedness of all life. This sense of connection fosters a sense of empathy and compassion, encouraging us to care for the environment and each other. Nature, in essence, helps us

CHAPTER 12: THE BEAUTY OF NATURE

see the bigger picture and recognize our place in the world.

13

Chapter 13: The Strength of Community

Community plays a vital role in our well-being and sense of belonging. By fostering connections and building supportive networks, we can create a strong foundation that helps us navigate life's challenges. Community provides us with a sense of belonging, purpose, and mutual support, enhancing our overall quality of life.

One of the key benefits of community is its ability to provide support and encouragement. In times of difficulty, having a strong support network can make a significant difference. By surrounding ourselves with people who care about us and understand our experiences, we can find comfort and strength. This support helps us stay resilient and motivated, allowing us to overcome obstacles and achieve our goals.

Another important aspect of community is its ability to foster a sense of belonging. Being part of a community gives us a sense of identity and purpose. It connects us to something larger than ourselves, providing meaning and direction in our lives. By participating in community activities and building relationships, we can create a sense of belonging that enhances our well-being and happiness.

Moreover, community promotes collaboration and collective growth. By working together towards common goals, we can achieve more than we could individually. This collaboration fosters a sense of unity and shared purpose, encouraging us to support and uplift each other. Community, in essence,

CHAPTER 13: THE STRENGTH OF COMMUNITY

helps us realize our potential and create positive change in the world around us.

14

Chapter 14: The Influence of Technology

Technology has transformed modern life in countless ways, shaping how we connect, communicate, and interact with the world. While technology offers numerous benefits, it also presents challenges that require careful consideration and balance. By understanding the impact of technology and using it mindfully, we can harness its potential to enhance our lives.

One of the key benefits of technology is its ability to connect us with others. Through digital communication platforms, we can maintain relationships, collaborate on projects, and share information across distances. This connectivity fosters a sense of global community and allows us to engage with diverse perspectives and ideas. However, it's important to balance digital interactions with in-person connections to maintain a sense of authenticity and depth in our relationships.

Another important aspect of technology is its role in facilitating access to information and knowledge. The internet provides us with a wealth of resources and learning opportunities, enabling us to expand our understanding and skills. By leveraging technology for education and personal growth, we can stay informed and adaptable in a rapidly changing world. However, it's essential to critically evaluate the information we encounter and avoid falling into the trap of misinformation.

Moreover, technology can enhance our productivity and creativity. With

CHAPTER 14: THE INFLUENCE OF TECHNOLOGY

the help of digital tools and applications, we can streamline tasks, manage projects, and explore new creative avenues. This empowerment allows us to achieve our goals more efficiently and pursue our passions with greater ease. However, it's important to set boundaries and avoid becoming overly reliant on technology, ensuring that we maintain a healthy balance between digital and offline activities.

15

Chapter 15: The Practice of Self-Compassion

Self-compassion is the practice of treating ourselves with kindness, understanding, and acceptance. By cultivating self-compassion, we can improve our mental and emotional well-being, build resilience, and enhance our overall quality of life. It involves acknowledging our imperfections and treating ourselves with the same care and empathy that we would offer to a friend.

One of the key benefits of self-compassion is its ability to reduce self-criticism and negative self-talk. By approaching ourselves with kindness and understanding, we can create a more supportive and nurturing inner dialogue. This shift in perspective allows us to recognize our inherent worth and value, fostering a sense of self-acceptance and self-love.

Another important aspect of self-compassion is its impact on our resilience. When we treat ourselves with compassion, we are better equipped to navigate challenges and setbacks. Instead of being harsh and judgmental, we can offer ourselves encouragement and support. This resilience helps us stay motivated and optimistic, allowing us to overcome obstacles and pursue our goals with confidence.

Moreover, self-compassion enhances our relationships with others. By treating ourselves with kindness and empathy, we become more attuned to the needs and experiences of those around us. This heightened awareness fosters a sense of empathy and compassion, enabling us to build stronger and more meaningful connections. Self-compassion, in essence, helps us create a more compassionate and caring world.

16

Chapter 16: The Journey of Lifelong Learning

Lifelong learning is the ongoing pursuit of knowledge and personal growth throughout our lives. By embracing a mindset of continuous learning, we can stay curious, adaptable, and engaged with the world around us. Lifelong learning enriches our lives, expands our horizons, and helps us navigate the complexities of modern life.

One of the key benefits of lifelong learning is its ability to keep our minds active and engaged. By continually seeking out new knowledge and experiences, we can maintain mental agility and cognitive function. This mental stimulation promotes overall well-being and helps us stay sharp and focused as we age. Lifelong learning also fosters a sense of curiosity and wonder, keeping our minds open to new possibilities and ideas.

Another important aspect of lifelong learning is its role in personal and professional development. By acquiring new skills and knowledge, we can enhance our abilities and stay competitive in the job market. This ongoing growth allows us to adapt to changing circumstances and seize new opportunities. Lifelong learning also helps us discover new passions and interests, enriching our lives and providing a sense of purpose and fulfillment.

Moreover, lifelong learning fosters a sense of connection and community. By participating in learning activities and sharing our knowledge with others, we can build relationships and create a sense of belonging. This collaborative learning environment encourages mutual support and growth, enhancing our overall well-being. Lifelong learning, in essence, helps us stay connected to the world and the people around us.

17

Chapter 17: The Quiet Revolution

The quiet revolution is a movement that embraces the power of solitude, curiosity, and resilience to redefine modern life. It's a journey of self-discovery and personal growth that challenges the status quo and encourages us to live more authentically and purposefully. By valuing introspection, continuous learning, and meaningful connections, we can create a more fulfilling and balanced existence.

At the heart of the quiet revolution is the belief that true fulfillment comes from within. It's about reconnecting with ourselves, exploring our passions, and embracing our unique strengths and talents. This journey of self-discovery allows us to align our actions with our values and create a life that is true to who we are. The quiet revolution encourages us to prioritize our well-being, nurture our relationships, and pursue our dreams with confidence and resilience.

The quiet revolution also recognizes the importance of community and collaboration. By building supportive networks and fostering meaningful connections, we can create a sense of belonging and mutual support. This sense of community enhances our well-being and helps us navigate the challenges of modern life. The quiet revolution encourages us to work together towards common goals, creating positive change in the world around us.

Ultimately, the quiet revolution is a call to live with intention and purpose.

It's a reminder that we have the power to shape our lives and create a fulfilling and meaningful existence. By embracing the principles of solitude, curiosity, and resilience, we can redefine modern life and create a brighter future for ourselves and the world around us.

Book Description

In a world increasingly defined by constant connectivity and relentless pace, "**The Quiet Revolution: How Solitude, Curiosity, and Resilience Redefine Modern Life**" offers a refreshing perspective on the power of introspection, exploration, and adaptability. This transformative guide explores how three fundamental principles—solitude, curiosity, and resilience—can help us navigate the complexities of modern life and cultivate a more fulfilling and balanced existence.

Through seventeen insightful chapters, the book delves into the myriad ways solitude can foster creativity and self-awareness, how curiosity fuels innovation and personal growth, and the role resilience plays in overcoming challenges and embracing change. Each chapter combines compelling narratives, practical strategies, and thought-provoking insights to encourage readers to embark on their own journey of self-discovery and transformation.

In "The Quiet Revolution," readers will learn to:

- Embrace solitude as a source of inner strength and creativity.
- Cultivate curiosity to explore new horizons and foster continuous learning.
- Develop resilience to adapt and thrive in the face of adversity.
- Find balance between work and play, prioritizing self-care and meaningful connections.
- Harness the power of mindfulness, gratitude, and simplicity to enhance well-being.
- Connect with nature and community to foster a sense of belonging and purpose.

Ultimately, this book is an invitation to redefine modern life by valuing introspection, nurturing curiosity, and building resilience. It's a call to live with intention and authenticity, creating a brighter future for ourselves and the world around us.

www.ingramcontent.com/pod-product-compliance
Lightning Source LLC
LaVergne TN
LVHW020501080526
838202LV00057B/6085